DREADFUL DISASTER

HIDEOUS HISTORY

CONTENTS

PAGE 4	PIECES OF THE PAST
PAGE 6	DINOSAUR DISASTER
PAGE 8	THE PARTYING PRINCE
PAGE 10	CHANGING MINDS
PAGE 12	LONDON'S BURNING
PAGE 14	ICEBERG INCIDENT
PAGE 16	THE RISE OF THE HUMANS
PAGE 18	BURSTING BANKS
PAGE 20	CLOUDY WITH A CHANCE OF CLOUD
PAGE 22	SWARM
PAGE 24	FROZEN IN TIME

PAGE 26   THE SPLIT

PAGE 28   THE EIGHT-MONTH ERUPTION

PAGE 30   HIDEOUS HISTORY

PAGE 31   GLOSSARY

PAGE 32   INDEX

Words that look like this are explained in the glossary on page 31.

Photo Credits
Images are courtesy of Shutterstock.com. With thanks to Getty Images, Thinkstock Photo and iStockphoto.
Front Cover – Everett Collection, Vadim Sadovski. 4–5 – PhotoJuli86, Romolo Tavani, KingVector, johavel. 6–7 – solarseven, Eva Kali, Herschel Hoffmeyer, Kakigori Studio. 8–9 – Everett Collection, Meganom. 10–11 – Rolf E. Staerk, Naypong Studio, elena castaldi viora, Steve Heap. 12–13 – Ben Gingell, Antoine Buchet, Miraphoto, Gaidamashchuk. 14–15 – Multigon. 16–17 – Dotted Yeti, Standret, Daniel Eskridge, Peyker, NYgraphic. 18–19 – Mo Wu, Yanfei Sun, baldezh. 20–21 – M. Rinandar Tasya, Masi Perez, Sabelskaya. 22–23 – ivanoel, Protasov AN, ianakauri. 24–25 – Alican Ozkeskin, BlackMac, Marcin Babul. 26–27 – Vagabjorn, YegoroV, Mopic, Dolvalol. 28–29 – africa2008st, Supatsara Ratchanet, common human. 30 – Mgr. Nobody.

BookLife PUBLISHING

©2023
BookLife Publishing Ltd.
King's Lynn, Norfolk
PE30 4LS, UK

All rights reserved.
Printed in Poland.

A catalogue record for this book is available from the British Library.

ISBN: 978-1-80155-892-1

Written by:
William Anthony

Edited by:
Hermione Redshaw

Designed by:
Drue Rintoul

All facts, statistics, web addresses and URLs in this book were verified as valid and accurate at time of writing. No responsibility for any changes to external websites or references can be accepted by either the author or publisher.

PIECES OF THE PAST

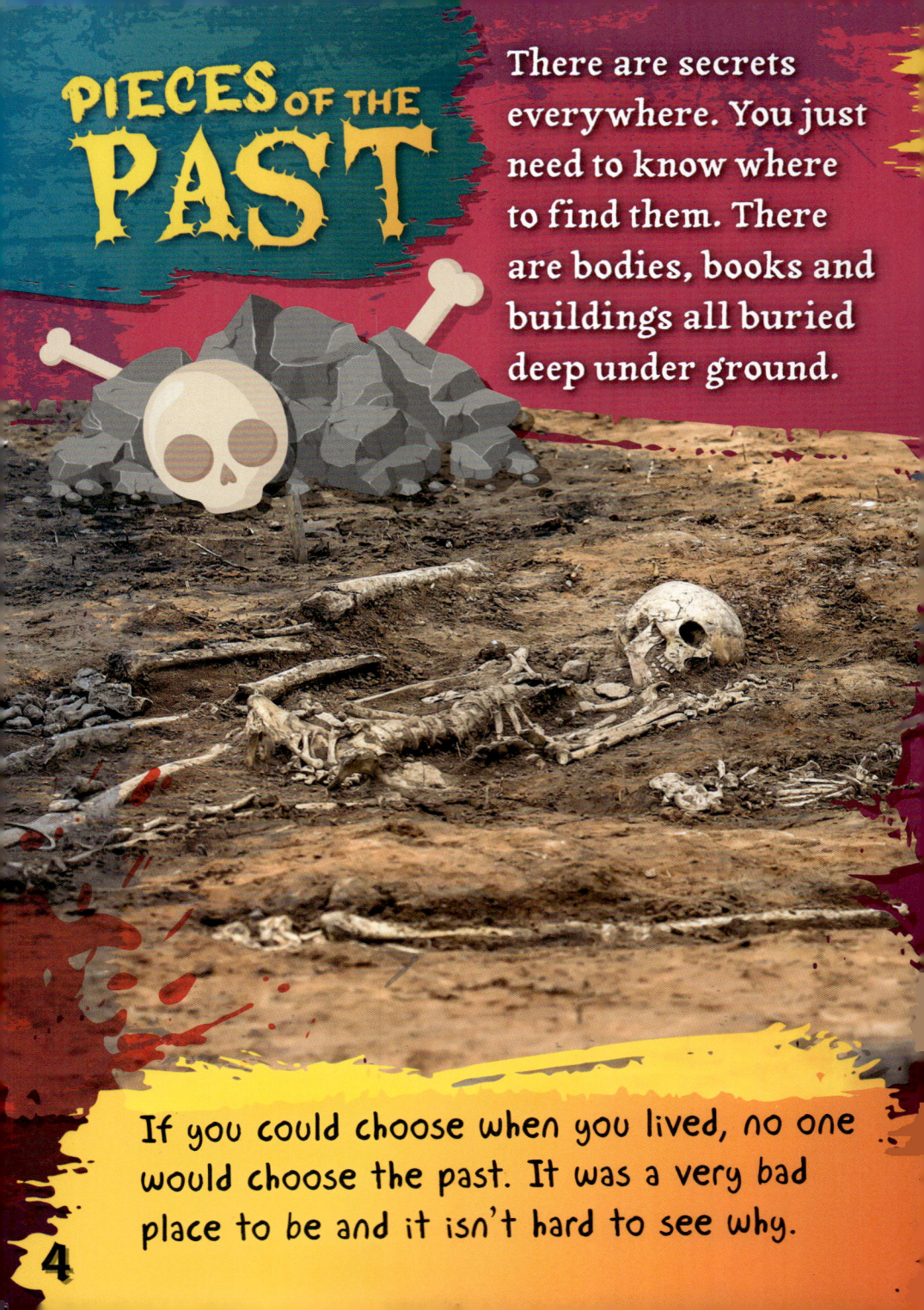

There are secrets everywhere. You just need to know where to find them. There are bodies, books and buildings all buried deep under ground.

If you could choose when you lived, no one would choose the past. It was a very bad place to be and it isn't hard to see why.

Wars and crimes were happening all around. People were always ill and a disaster was never too far away. Still, people got on with their lives.

Let's dive into the past. Are you properly prepared to lean about the hideous history of horrific disasters? You need to be a very brave soul...

DINOSAUR DISASTER

Dinosaurs are scary. They're big, they have gigantic teeth and their claws would rip a car in half. Yet, the disaster that wiped them off the planet was even scarier.

Some scientists think a colossal <u>asteroid</u> hit Earth around 65 million years ago. They say it caused huge amounts of dust to fill the air.

Other scientists think that huge volcanoes erupted and filled the air with <u>ash</u> clouds.

Whether it was an asteroid or a volcanic eruption, it was still terrifying. All the dust would have blocked out sunlight. Earth would have been cold and plants would have died.

Then, it would have got very hot. Animals, such as dinosaurs, wouldn't have been able to cope.

THE PARTYING PRINCE

King Henry I only had one heir to his throne. It was Prince William Adelin. However, Prince William never got to take the throne. Disaster got in the way.

KING HENRY I

King Henry picked out a special ship for Prince William to sail back from the battlefield on. Its name was the White Ship. The ship was filled with over 150 people.

The ship never made it home. It tried to leave France and struck a rock on the way. William and his crew were too busy partying to notice.

The ship sank and only one person survived. They swam back to tell everyone the bad news. After King Henry I died, people fought over the throne for many years.

CHANGING MINDS

Most disasters destroy things and cost people lots of money. Some disasters change how people think.

On the 1st of November 1775, lots of <u>Christians</u> in Lisbon were in church. Suddenly, everybody heard a big rumble and the ground began to shake.

One of the biggest earthquakes in Europe's history had hit Lisbon!

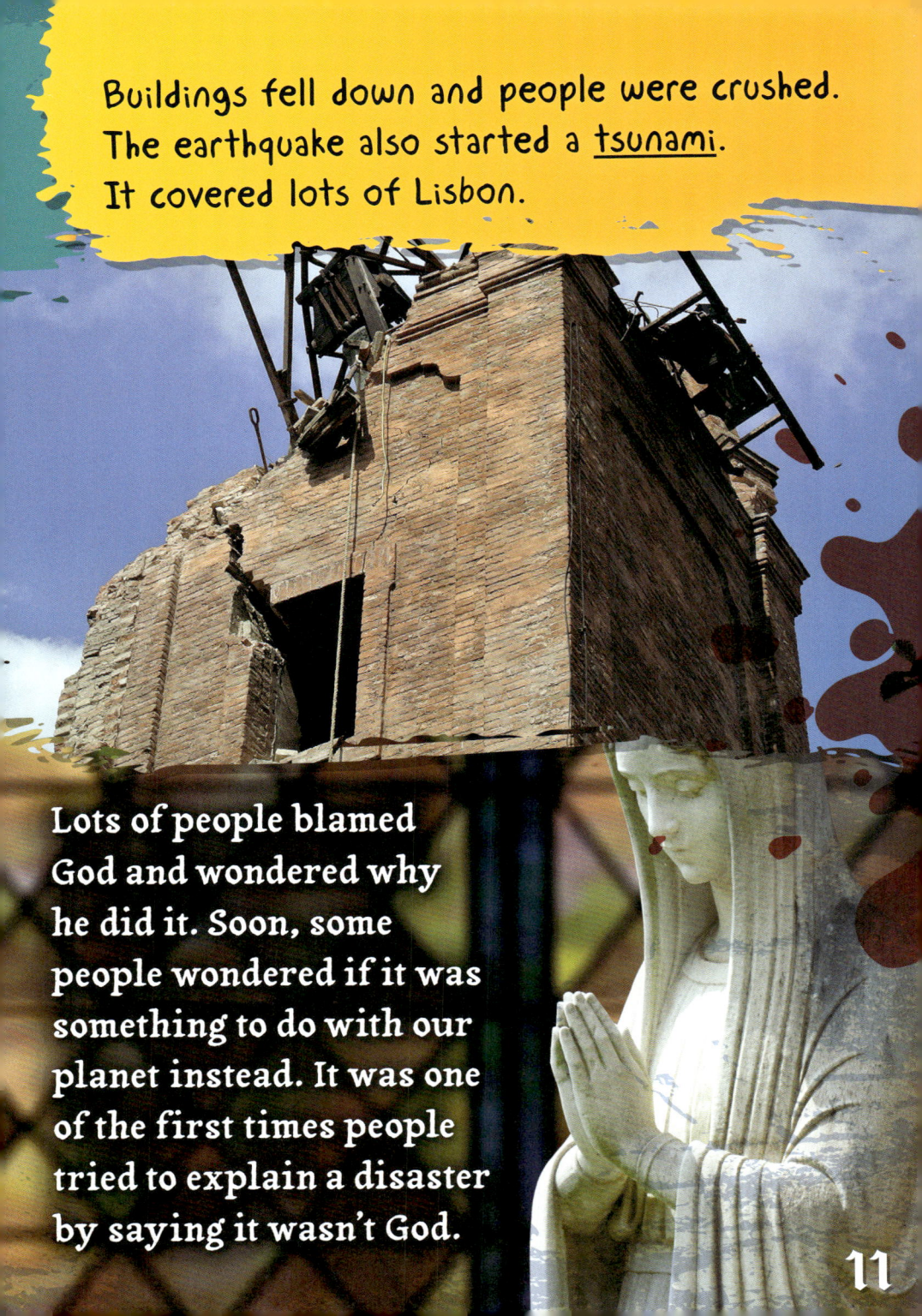

Buildings fell down and people were crushed. The earthquake also started a <u>tsunami</u>. It covered lots of Lisbon.

Lots of people blamed God and wondered why he did it. Soon, some people wondered if it was something to do with our planet instead. It was one of the first times people tried to explain a disaster by saying it wasn't God.

London's Burning

Sometimes, humans can cause the biggest disasters. In 1666, one baker accidentally started a fire that took over the city of London.

Thomas Farriner owned a bakery on Pudding Lane. One night, a spark flew out of his oven and started a fire in the bakery. There had been no rain, so all the wooden buildings were very dry.

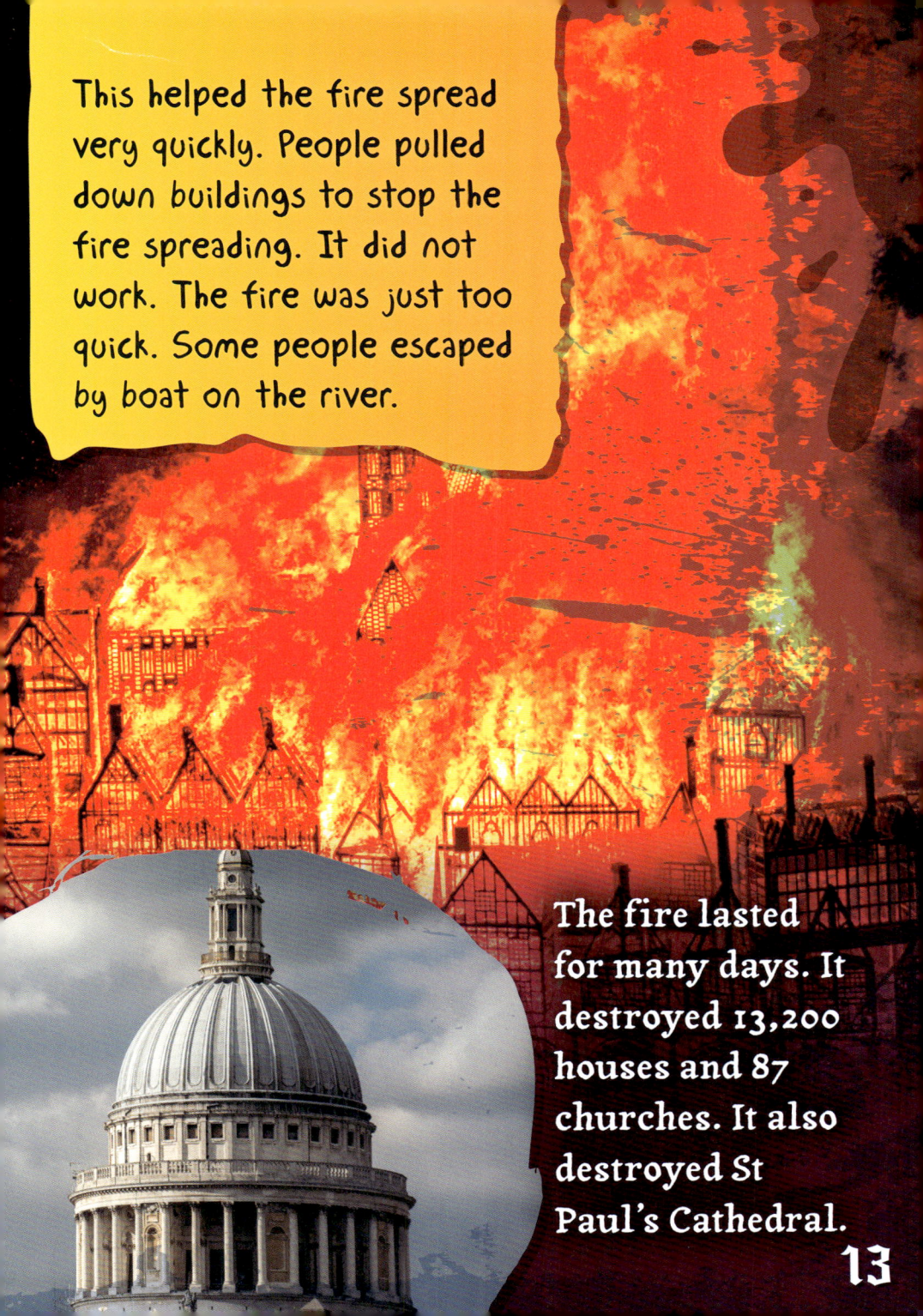

This helped the fire spread very quickly. People pulled down buildings to stop the fire spreading. It did not work. The fire was just too quick. Some people escaped by boat on the river.

The fire lasted for many days. It destroyed 13,200 houses and 87 churches. It also destroyed St Paul's Cathedral.

13

ICEBERG INCIDENT

People were very confident when they set sail on the Titanic. It was known as "The Unsinkable Ship". It was the biggest ship in the world in 1912.

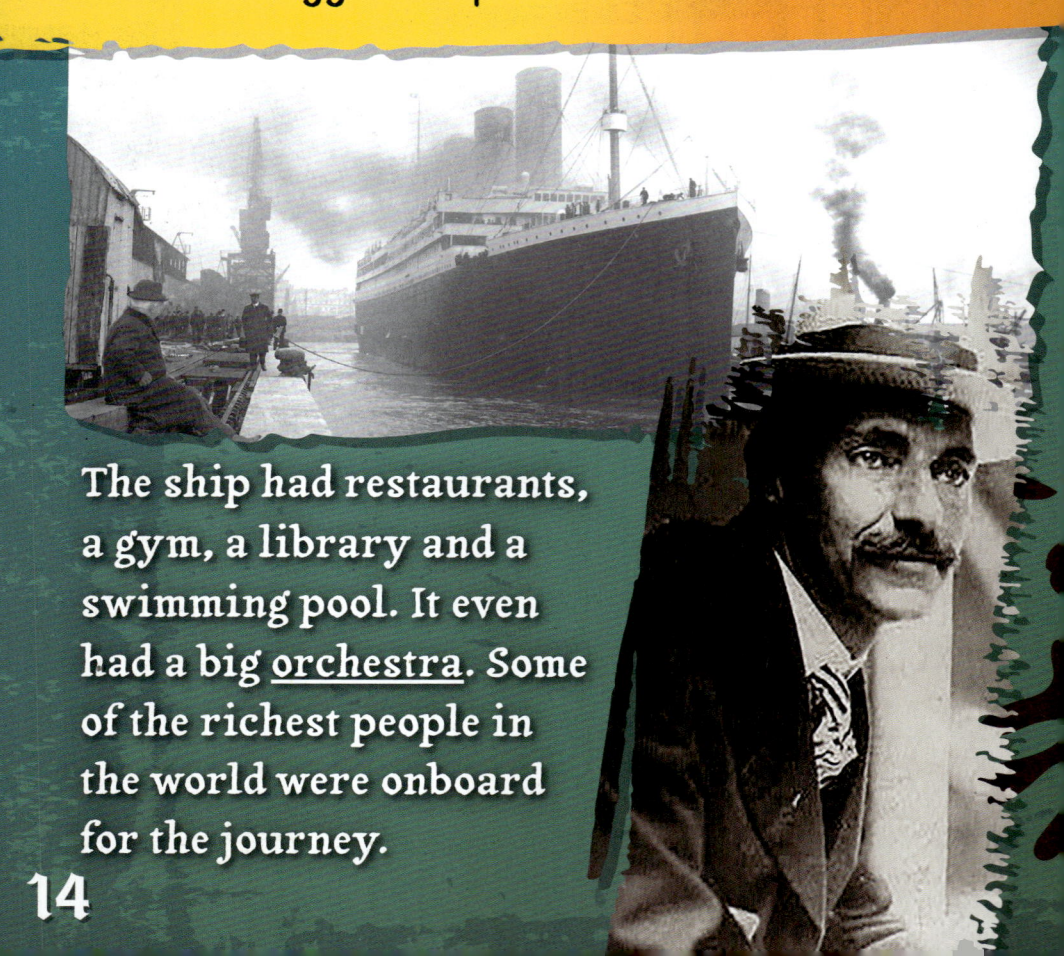

The ship had restaurants, a gym, a library and a swimming pool. It even had a big <u>orchestra</u>. Some of the richest people in the world were onboard for the journey.

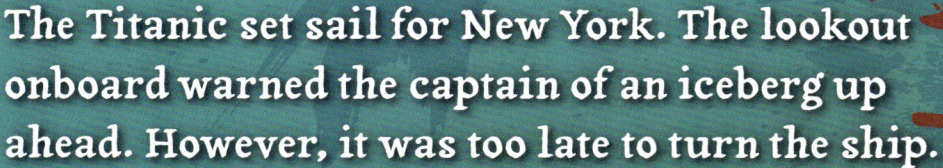

The Titanic set sail for New York. The lookout onboard warned the captain of an iceberg up ahead. However, it was too late to turn the ship.

Iceberg, right ahead!

The ship hit the iceberg hard. The Titanic was ruined and began to sink. It took two hours to disappear. More than 1,500 people died on that fateful night.

THE RISE OF THE HUMANS

The Earth is always changing temperature. It can be very hot for millions of years. Then, it can turn very cold for millions of years. The coldest periods are called ice ages.

There are times when ice covers more of the world than usual. This is a big disaster for any animals and plants that can't <u>adapt</u> quickly enough.

The last big ice age ended around 10,000 years ago. There were woolly mammoths and sabre-toothed tigers. Ice ages were difficult for lots of animals.

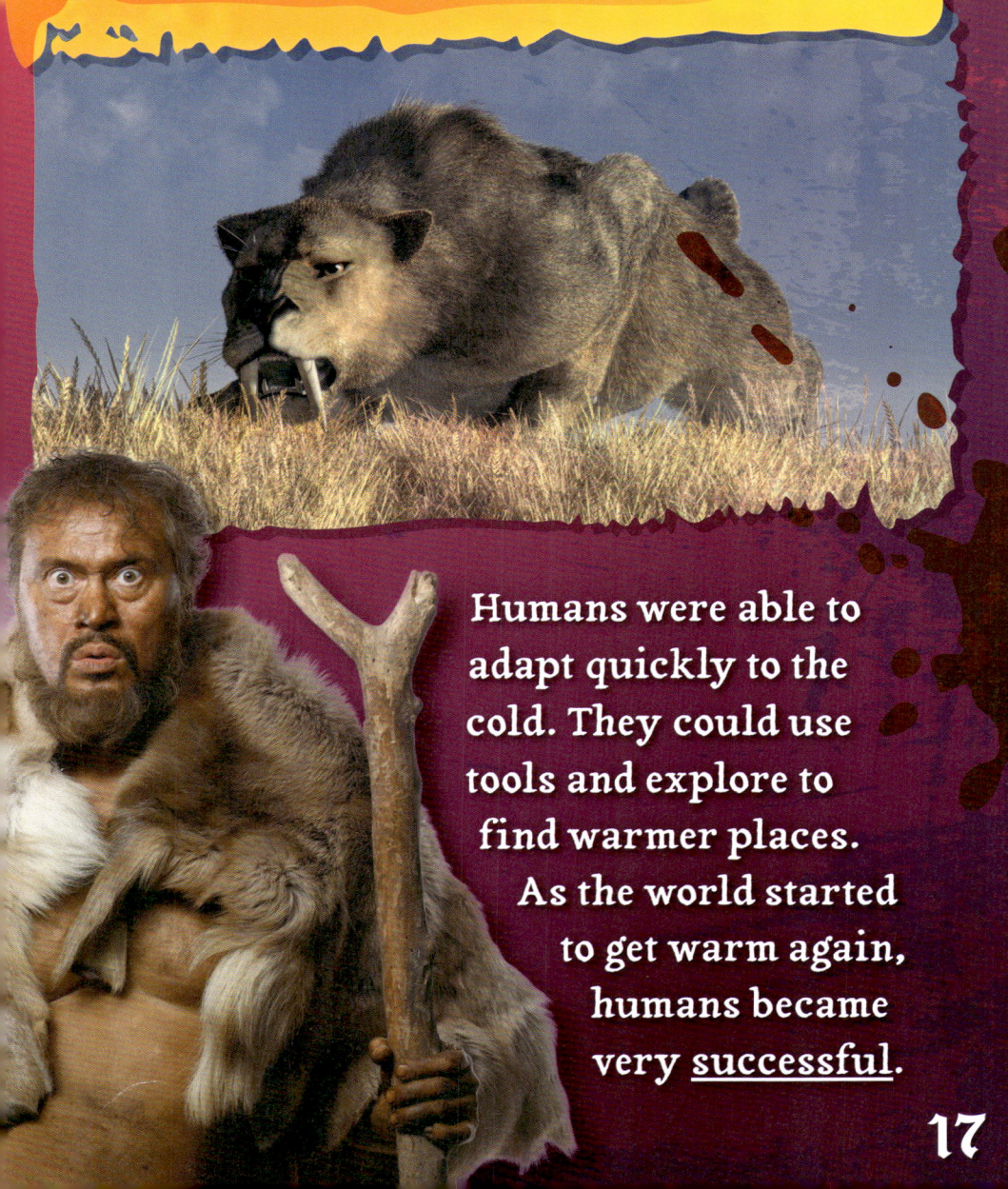

Humans were able to adapt quickly to the cold. They could use tools and explore to find warmer places. As the world started to get warm again, humans became very <u>successful</u>.

BURSTING BANKS

Disasters are often <u>ranked</u> by how many people die. There is nothing nice about it, but that's hideous history for you. One of the deadliest disasters happened in China in 1887.

The second-longest river in China flooded. It is called the Yellow River. The Yellow River flooded often. However, this flood was much worse than normal.

The flood in 1887 destroyed 11 large towns and hundreds of villages. It is thought that at least 900,000 people died. People climbed on houses and trees to escape the flood.

People continued to live by rivers like the Yellow River. They were good for farming and provided food and <u>transport</u>. People took the risk for the reward.

CLOUDY WITH A CHANCE OF CLOUD

The summer of 1816 was not like other summers. It was very cold and there was snow. Plants did not grow well. It all happened because a giant volcano erupted.

Please don't explode!

Mount Tambora is a volcano in Indonesia. It exploded twice in 1815. It was so loud that the second eruption could be heard hundreds of kilometres away.

It was the biggest explosion ever to happen on Earth. Smoke and ash filled the sky above. The volcano made a sort of fog spread around the planet.

The fog blocked lots of sunlight from reaching the ground. Earth was much colder that summer because the Sun could not warm it up!

21

SWARM

Look at this little animal. It is a locust. Does it look like a disaster? What do you mean, no? Think again!

Locusts are a big problem for farmers all over the world. They fly around eating all sorts of things planted by farmers. People in North America found out just how much of a problem they were in 1875.

Millions of locusts gathered together in a group called a swarm. The swarms looked like huge clouds. They ate thousands of plants and even got inside people's houses.

Lots of people left their homes for good to escape the swarms. Many people did not have food because the farms had nothing left after the locusts!

23

FROZEN IN TIME

In Italy, there is a city that is frozen in time. Its name is Pompeii. Nobody lives there anymore. Yet, the town still stands in place.

Statues still stand tall. People's furniture hasn't moved for almost 2,000 years. You can see <u>casts</u> of people moments before they died all those years ago. But how?

Pompeii was a busy city near a volcano called Mount Vesuvius. In AD 79, the volcano exploded. It created a cloud of ash and smoke over 32 kilometres high in the air.

The ashy powder rained down on the city. The lava and ash that covered the city and people kept everything perfectly in place. We can see those things today!

THE SPLIT

Aleppo is a city in Syria that still stands today. Yet, it went through a huge earthquake in 1138. Lots of Aleppo was destroyed by the earthquake.

Buildings collapsed and people were crushed. Some of the nearby villages were also affected. People at the time said the ground split in half beneath their feet.

Aleppo is very unlucky when it comes to earthquakes. This is because it sits on something called a fault line. A fault line is where two tectonic plates meet.

Tectonic plates are huge slabs of rock that make up the Earth's surface. They move and bump into each other. This makes earthquakes happen. People didn't know this in 1138!

THE EIGHT-MONTH ERUPTION

Laki is a group of volcanoes in Iceland. In 1783, one of the biggest eruptions in recent history took place. It wasn't just one big bang. It lasted for eight months!

The volcanoes gave off lots of things during those eight months. One of those things was sulphur. Sulphur is something dangerous that can become part of the air.

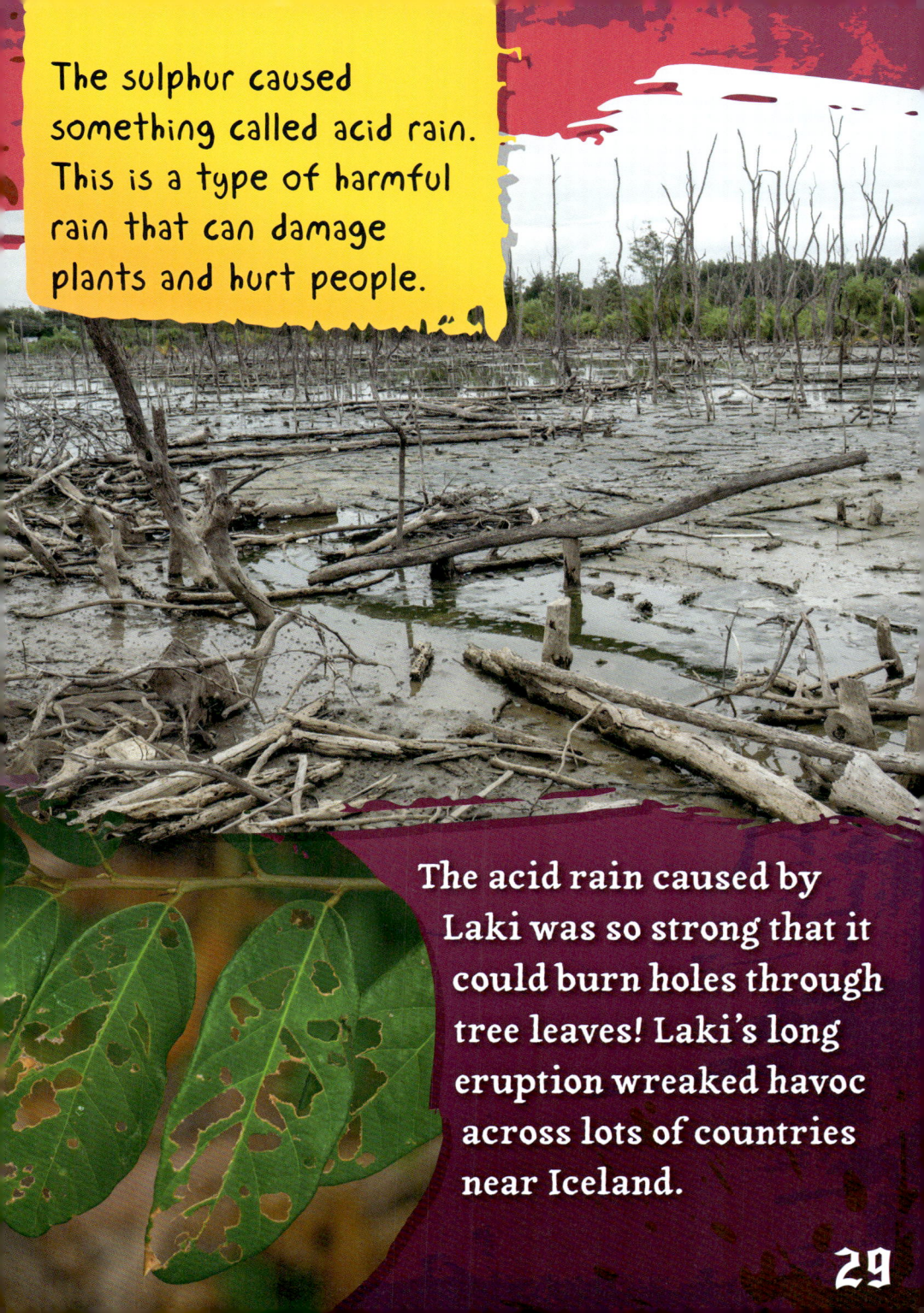

The sulphur caused something called acid rain. This is a type of harmful rain that can damage plants and hurt people.

The acid rain caused by Laki was so strong that it could burn holes through tree leaves! Laki's long eruption wreaked havoc across lots of countries near Iceland.

HIDEOUS HISTORY

You can relax now. Let your heart calm down. The past was a terrifying place, but you do not live there now.

These stories just go to show that no matter where you live, no one is safe from a disaster.

GLOSSARY

ADAPT change over a long period of time

ASH a powdery material left behind after something is burnt

ASTEROID a type of very large rock that can be found in space

CASTS objects created by a material hardening over or in something else

CHRISTIANS people who believe in the religion of Christianity

ORCHESTRA a group of musicians who play a variety of musical instruments together

RANKED put in order from smallest to biggest

SUCCESSFUL when someone or something has done well

TRANSPORT all the ways in which people travel from place to place

TSUNAMI a very high and powerful wave in the ocean, which is usually caused by an earthquake under the water

INDEX

ACID RAIN 29
ASTEROIDS 6–7
EARTHQUAKES 10–11, 26–27
FIRES 12–13
ICE AGES 16–17
LOCUSTS 22–23
RIVERS 13, 18–19
SHIPS 8–9, 14–15
TECTONIC PLATES 27
TSUNAMIS 11
VOLCANOES 7, 20–21, 25, 28

AN INTRODUCTION TO BOOKLIFE RAPID READERS...

Packed full of gripping topics and twisted tales, BookLife Rapid Readers are perfect for older children looking to propel their reading up to top speed. With three levels based on our planet's fastest animals, children will be able to find the perfect point from which to accelerate their reading journey. From the spooky to the silly, these roaring reads will turn every child at every reading level into a prolific page-turner!

CHEETAH
The fastest animals on land, cheetahs will be taking their first strides as they race to top speed.

MARLIN
The fastest animals under water, marlins will be blasting through their journey.

FALCON
The fastest animals in the air, falcons will be flying at top speed as they tear through the skies.